Super Brady:
Always on the Move!

Written and Illustrated by Brady and his 4th Grade Friends

at Spring Garden Elementary School
in Bethlehem, Pennsylvania

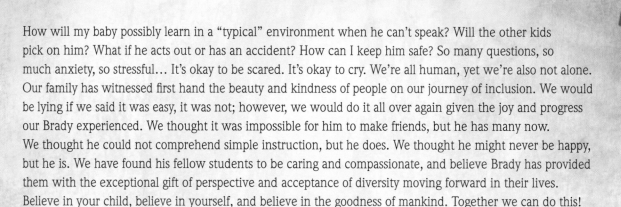

How will my baby possibly learn in a "typical" environment when he can't speak? Will the other kids pick on him? What if he acts out or has an accident? How can I keep him safe? So many questions, so much anxiety, so stressful… It's okay to be scared. It's okay to cry. We're all human, yet we're also not alone. Our family has witnessed first hand the beauty and kindness of people on our journey of inclusion. We would be lying if we said it was easy, it was not; however, we would do it all over again given the joy and progress our Brady experienced. We thought it was impossible for him to make friends, but he has many now. We thought he could not comprehend simple instruction, but he does. We thought he might never be happy, but he is. We have found his fellow students to be caring and compassionate, and believe Brady has provided them with the exceptional gift of perspective and acceptance of diversity moving forward in their lives. Believe in your child, believe in yourself, and believe in the goodness of mankind. Together we can do this!

— *Chuck Strom (Brady's dad)*

We have been filled with so much thankfulness and love for the way that Brady's classmates have so effortlessly and selflessly included him. They see Brady for who he is before his disability. While Brady cannot speak, his friends never forget that he can hear. They know he hears when they ask him to play, share their laughter, or be a part of their team. Inclusion to Brady means breaking the silence that surrounds him. It is about acceptance and how the smallest act of kindness from one person can mean the world to another. It's about loving and caring for one another. We remain hopeful that one day Brady will be able to speak, and know that he will call his classmates his true super heroes!

— *Kim Strom (Brady's mom)*

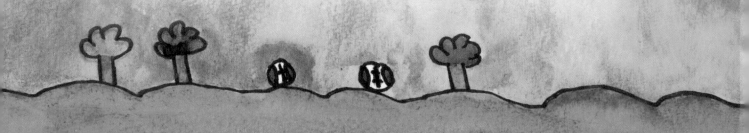

ISBN: 978-0-692-06007-0
First Edition, 2018

We dedicate this book
to Brady
because he inspires us
to be a friend
to everyone.

Mikayla's Voice
PO Box 232, Nazareth, PA 18064
www.mikaylasvoice.org

On the first day of fourth grade,

I was happy to see my friends.

We all talk to each other,

but one of our friends cannot.

Brady doesn't speak.

We didn't know how to feel when we first met Brady.

We thought he was very different than us.

Most of us felt shy.

Some of us were afraid.

Others were not scared at all,

just curious because we never had a friend like Brady.

We were all confused about why he didn't talk

and was running around.

What did he think of us?

I met Brady in second grade when he sat at my table.

I was nervous but I said, "hi."

He said "hello" back to me by pressing a button

on a box the size and shape of an iPad®.

The next day I asked Brady why he couldn't talk

and his helper said he has autism.

She said he uses an electronic communication device to talk.

The words on the buttons are pre-recorded

so when Brady pushes a button on his device, it speaks for him.

We love to talk to Brady on his device.

Sometimes he will say something silly and make us laugh.

He is funny, generous, and kind.

Anyone could just walk up and play with Brady,

and once you are friends with him, you are always friends with him.

He is the best friend ever.

We have learned a lot about autism since meeting Brady.

One out of 68 people have autism.

It is a disability that often makes it hard to communicate.

Things that we find easy may be difficult for kids with autism,

and some have behaviors that they repeat all the time.

No one person has the same type of autism.

For Brady, autism means he loves to fidget and move around.

He is not able to talk, but other kids with autism can.

Caroline's brother talks as much as we do.

Delyla knows a little boy who has autism and can speak,

but only says a few words at a time.

He loves trains and always talks about them.

Some kids copy stuff we say or

repeat what they have heard on television or in movies.

Brady has made a lot of progress since he started

kindergarten at Spring Garden Elementary School.

He used to yell in the library when

he wanted something but couldn't explain.

Brady could not communicate because

he didn't get his device until second grade.

Since he couldn't say what he wanted,

he ended up yelling to get attention.

Before he had a communication device,

Brady also used to throw himself on the floor when he was really mad.

He had tantrums because he was frustrated or misunderstood.

What if you wanted to tell someone something, but you couldn't say it?

Brady doesn't have tantrums or yell anymore

because he has a device and knows how to communicate better.

If you ask Brady a question,

he can press a button to answer "yes" or "no."

Brady's device also has buttons that say words for him

like actions, names, foods, and now sentences!

When he presses a picture of two people playing it will say,

"I want to play."

He can also ask for help.

His helper added our pictures to his device

so Brady can pick and communicate which friend

he wants to play with or get help from.

We think it's really cool when
Brady pushes a button on his device and it talks.
Brady is good at finding things on his device,
but it can be challenging.
It has a ton of boxes with words and pictures
so sometimes he presses the wrong button.

Brady let us try it once and it is really confusing.

He would give us something to find on it.

For instance the card said McDonald's®.

You had to find and press, "eat," then "place," then "McDonald's."

Brady has also learned to talk with us

in other ways besides using his device.

He has lots of awesome ways

to communicate with all his friends.

If he wants to say "hello," he comes up to you

and acts very excited to see you.

He goes on his tippy toes,

wiggles his hands like crazy,

and smiles at you.

His smile is very nice.

When Brady feels hungry he puts his hand on his tummy,

runs and gets his lunchbox, and gives it to you.

Sometimes his helper gives him a pack of Skittles®

to hold him over until it is time to eat lunch.

When Brady wants to go to the bathroom,

he will go to the door and look at his helper

or push the button on his device that says, "Bathroom."

If he really needs to go, Brady will make his device say,

"Bathroom, bathroom, bathroom" about ten times!

When we have to use the bathroom,

we raise our hand and ask our teacher to go.

If she doesn't see us or we have to go badly,

we wiggle and squirm in our seat,

start waving our hands really hard, or go up and ask her.

We are saying exactly the same thing.

When he jumps up and down, that means he is happy.

If Brady is angry or upset, he makes noise

and bangs his water bottle on his desk.

This doesn't bother us.

It has helped us learn to be focused.

Autism can make it hard for Brady to focus on his work.

To get some energy out and help him focus,

Brady will fidget with things and walk around the classroom.

Sometimes Brady walks around a lot.

He will go up when the teacher is speaking,

but we help him get back to where he is supposed to be.

He even walked out of our classroom when no one was looking

but his helper brought him back to class.

In case Brady should ever leave our school, his house,

or get lost in a crowd, he wears two bracelets.

One says he has autism and the other looks like a watch.

It is a tracking bracelet that would help his parents and the police

find him if he wandered off and was lost.

Brady also wears a third bracelet that plays a song from *Superman*.

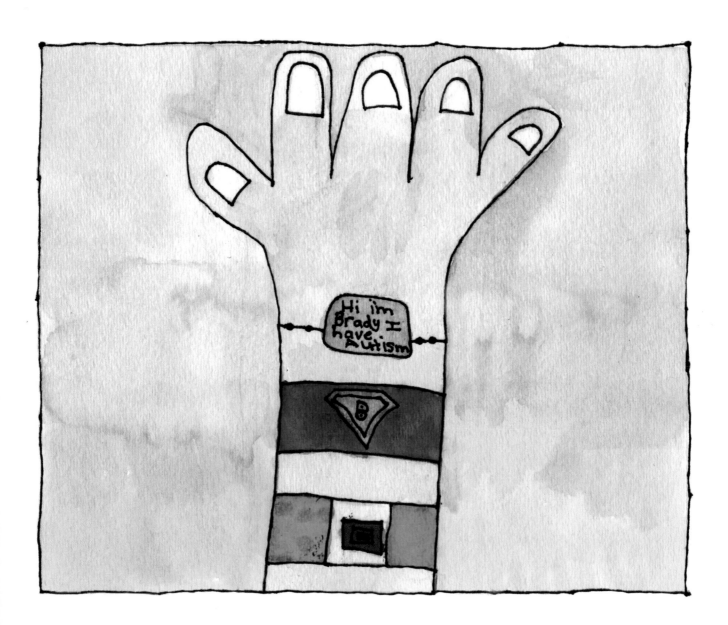

Since Brady likes to move around and jump,

at recess we go on the playground bouncy bridge to bounce.

We all went to his hero-themed birthday parties

at "BounceU" and "FreeFall Trampoline Park."

Brady loves trampolines and super heroes.

We had so much fun!

My 8th birthday party was at the "Skateaway" roller rink.

Brady uses the same skates as I do and might skate better than me.

Our class went bowling on a field trip and we've seen Brady

at Freedom and Liberty High School football games.

Brady loves to be busy and keep moving.

Brady moves differently than us in many ways.

He wiggles his fingers, shakes his hands, and waves his arms a lot.

Sometimes he stands and walks on his toes.

He always has more energy to his step

and when Brady hears music, he sways back and forth.

We call it the "Brady dance."

Brady loves music and plays in

our school's hand bell choir.

They meet every Wednesday before school

and play in our school concerts.

Brady plays one of the lowest bells,

which is the biggest hand chime.

Brady is also good at baseball and swimming.

His friend Julia watches his baseball games and cheers him on.

Brady has an inground pool in his backyard

and swims in his pool almost everyday in the summer.

He swims on pool floats with his friends and sister,

but he can also swim in the deep end of the pool without any help.

Everyday in school Brady gets help from our teacher, Mrs. Wagner,

and his two helpers, Miss Erin and Miss Donna.

Miss Erin helps Brady eat lunch and

Miss Donna helps him with his education.

Mrs. Wagner comes over and has Brady show her what he can do.

Brady learns the same subjects and topics as us, but in a different way.

Brady understands better by using stuff that he can touch.

He learns "greater and less than" with Fruit Loops® cereal.

Out of two bowls, he picks which one has more or less cereal.

Brady learns fractions by using pieces of a paper pizza.

When some of the slices are taken away,

he looks for the fraction on his device.

Miss Donna helps him with our math facts.

We play a game with division and

Brady uses his device to find the answer.

Sometimes when we have teams in math,

he gets the winning point.

Brady learns vocabulary by matching words to show meaning.

If you ask "Is January a holiday?" Brady hits "No" on his device.

If you ask "Is Easter?" then he hits "Yes!"

Brady also has to match his vocabulary words

with pictures to show the definitions.

In Social Studies, he uses task cards and matches states and regions.

When we are reading, Brady has the same book on his iPad.

His iPad reads to him and his group

so he can still hear the story we're reading.

Sometimes the book on the iPad also has a video to watch.

Or we read with Brady.

We encourage Brady when he is doing something hard.
We show him where the hanger is for his coat and bookbag,
and remind him to sit down when he has to.
We help him stay in line when we are walking down the hall
and take him up to get his lunch.

Brady helps us too.

At lunch, he gives me a napkin if I don't have one.

If I'm having a bad day, he will give me a high five and cheer me up.

Brady makes me and my friends laugh by doing funny things.

He helps us by making the school day go by faster than usual.

I love being friends with Brady

because he is a very good friend back.

Brady's friendship is very, very important to us.

He's taught us to respect everybody and made me a better person.

Now we won't be shy when we meet people with autism,

or any other disability.

Brady has inspired us to be friends with everyone!

Mikayla's Voice was founded on the belief that children are in the best position to teach our community about the importance of inclusion and the celebration of diversity.

For too many years, people with disabilities have been excluded from social, educational, and employment opportunities. Most adults remember when all children with disabilities were placed in separate classrooms. Until becoming Mikayla's mom, I never really knew anyone with a disability. So I understand. Fear is the greatest barrier to inclusion. When people are afraid to do or say the wrong thing, sometimes it keeps them from doing the right thing. Parents hush their children and whisk them away, rather than suggest they just say "hello." Teachers don't volunteer to include a child with autism because they are unsure about his communication needs. Parents themselves are afraid their child won't be accepted by his non-disabled peers.

Fear not. Children have always been the most accepting of Mikayla's disabilities. Thanks to increased inclusive practices in our schools and communities, this generation of children has been blessed with greater appreciation for and friendships with children with disabilities. For most, it is still a new experience. They might be unsure, even nervous, but children are born without bias, less inclined to judgment, and more likely to ask questions. Unless taught otherwise, kids are kind.

Understanding, compassionate, and accepting children grow into adults who celebrate diversity and embrace individuals of all abilities. True cultural change begins with our youth. Lessons learned early will remain with them for life to be shared with future generations. They are the future teachers who welcome all kids into their classroom, the parents who stop to introduce their child to another in a wheelchair, and the employer who sees a job applicant's skills before his walker.

Our children are our future and we are proud to give them a voice today…they are Mikayla's Voice. In addition to publishing children's books for other kids, Mikayla's Voice develops and coordinates unique and innovative programs that allow children with and without disabilities to work and play together. These programs are designed to showcase children's talent and creativity as they demonstrate successful inclusion in education, art, sports, and recreation. This builds their self-confidence, empowers them to stand up for what they believe, and encourages their growth into adults who continue to advocate for inclusion.

For more information, please visit us at
www.mikaylasvoice.org.